Run Faster Marathons

The Proven Path to PR

Chris Knighton

ISBN: 9798754441286

To Erica
for being there
every step of the way

Introduction

Welcome to *Run Faster Marathons: The Proven Path to PR*. My name is Coach Chris Knighton and I am the founder of *Knighton Runs Marathon Coaching*.

I grew up in Massachusetts, just south of Boston. I did not run when I was younger, but I remember clearly as a kid when my dad took me into the city to watch the Boston Marathon. We were standing on Boylston Street, just before Copley Square, as we saw the winners of the race come streaming in.

I remember their energy, the excitement of the crowd, and the sun shining down on us all. There are few experiences from my youth that I recall so vividly. From that day forward, I always dreamed of running the Boston Marathon myself.

In the years that followed, I dabbled with running but never went further than that. Then in my mid-twenties, I finally decided that if I was ever going to run the Boston Marathon, I had to start taking my running seriously, put in the work, and begin to train like an athlete.

This is when I learned that not just anyone can run Boston. It takes a seriously fast qualifying time in another marathon to even be considered for entry! So now, not only did I need to run another marathon before doing Boston, but I had to do it really, really fast.

At this point in my journey, I realized I honestly did not know what I was doing other than just going out and simply running. I saw some immediate success but did not know how to move forward from there. That is when I reached out to my first running coach. I asked her to help me train for my first marathon.

My coach taught me how to actually train like an athlete, not just a casual runner. I saw immediate results and the improvements I got kept coming and coming. I learned how to intelligently structure my training, put variation into the day-to-day, run my first speed workouts, complete long runs with ease, and build the confidence I needed to race to the best of my ability. She helped me not just BQ but go far beyond that.

I started *Knighton Runs Marathon Coaching* to share the life-changing power that working together as athlete-and-coach has with runners like you.

Over the years, It has been my honor and passion to help athletes run new PR's, win races, qualify for the Boston Marathon, and feel better about their running than ever before. I firmly believe that development and success in sport directly correlates to success in life as a whole. The skills we improve through running: discipline, patience, courage and confidence do not only make us better athletes. They make us better husbands, wives, sons, daughters, parents, friends, leaders, and teammates as well.

If we can run faster marathons, we can do anything.

In this book, I outline the key principles you need to know to achieve steady year-after-year improvement in your running.

Running at its heart is a simple sport, but the endless amount of information online and in books make it very confusing to understand what is the best approach. This book synthesizes the best concepts I have learned from studying many different philosophies and applying them to my athletes. *Run Faster Marathons* delivers only what you need to know to become a faster, healthier, and more consistent runner.

When you combine the lessons shared in this book with patience, hard work, and dedication, you will exceed your goals.

Enjoy the journey,
Coach Chris Knighton

Table of Contents

Essential Concepts for Marathon Success

The Six Phases of Marathon Training

Supplemental Practices to Go Beyond "Just Running"

Essential Concepts for
Marathon Success

1. Every Runner Must Ask This Question

Before you lace up your shoes and step outside, ask yourself,

"Why do I run?"

This is the single most important question you can ask yourself before embarking on months of challenging marathon training. We are competitive runners. We love to race, but race results are just the carrots that we chase. They are the reward at the end of a long journey. During the day in and day out of training, we do not catch the carrot. Instead, we build the rabbit.

It is the act of running itself, not racing, that makes up 99% of our sport. We must love the day in and day out to justify the 1% at the end. Your why is what makes you open up your front door and step outside. It is the satisfaction you receive from every easy run, hard workout, and long exploration you set off on.

Every runner has a different why

For me, the times I set and the competition I face are secondary to the reason I run. They are icing on the cake but not the bulk of what makes it taste so good. Just getting outside for easy runs and practicing my race-paces in workouts makes me feel like I am moving forward. The very process of training makes me feel empowered to take on any goal. It is the pursuit of ongoing improvement and the adventure I experience along the way that make up my why. When I run, I get a positive feeling of self-worth and know that I can do anything I set my heart to. That is why I run.

Maintaining your drive

All runners experience highs and lows in motivation and willpower. When we are in good spirits, we all say we love to run and will fight to the end in races. But during the low periods, it can be hard to even get out the door. When those inevitable lows strike, knowing our why is what makes all the hard work involved with running seem worthwhile.

Go deeply within

- *How does it make you feel when you go run?*
- *Why do you push at the end of a workout?*
- *How come you want to run more often, further, and faster?*
- *Do you get discouraged when your running goes poorly?*
- *How does it make you feel when you ace a workout?*
- *What do new PR's mean to you?*
- *Do the feelings you get from running affect the rest of your life?*

Write down and reflect on your why

Write your why down on paper. Say it out loud. Keep it around as a reminder. When the going gets tough, you will have your answer to keep pushing forward.

After every running milestone, pull out your piece of paper again. Read it and reflect on what you wrote. Does this why still ring true to you?

2. Running Rules to Live By

1. Give every run a purpose.

2. Stay comfortable on daily runs.

3. Run fast only when it counts.

4. Be consistent with your training.

5. Run on soft surfaces often.

6. Train with the seasons.

7. Sleep as much as you can.

8. Drink lots of water, eat lots of carbs.

9. Listen to your body, quiet your mind.

10. Do not try to rush fitness.

3. The Right Way to Increase Your Mileage

Mileage matters

Increasing your mileage is the best thing you can do to improve your running speed and endurance. But too many runners, coaches, and training plans do not go about it in the right way.

You must increase mileage carefully. If you increase it too quickly or do not simultaneously prioritize your recovery between runs, the increase in mileage will likely backfire in the form of injury or stagnation.

What is the optimal amount of mileage for you?

If your goal is to become the fastest runner you can be, then the optimal amount of mileage is the highest amount you can handle while still enjoying running and without getting hurt.

The key to increasing your weekly running mileage is to do it *gradually* and *patiently*.

Why mileage matters

Running more is the best thing you can do to become a better distance runner.

Running itself gives you all the physiological benefits you need to run faster and longer. All cross training and supplemental exercise is purely meant to allow you to run more and lower risk of injury. These activities do not necessarily make you a better runner by themselves.

By running more mileage, you spend more time on your feet. Your heart therefore spends more time pumping hard, building your aerobic engine ever more powerful. You stress and rebuild your skeletal-muscular system more, which in turn makes you a stronger athlete who can handle even more frequency and intensity.

There is a point for all athletes in which they hit their upper limit for mileage. Every individual can only handle so much mentally and physically, but until you get there, more mileage is very often the right answer.

Where building mileage goes wrong

One popular way of increasing mileage includes the well known *10% rule*, where you only increase mileage by 10% per week. The problem with this is that the math just does not work out in many cases. When following this approach, low mileage runners will hardly see their mileage increase at all, whereas higher mileage runners will increase their mileage too quickly. In addition to the exponential growth of mileage that the 10% rule implies, it also does not take into consideration the placement of periods of lower mileage that are essential for recovery.

Another popular approach, often taken by new marathoners is to simply lay out a long-run schedule, consisting of 16-milers, 18-milers, and 20-milers, and follow that trajectory regardless of its effect on the total weekly mileage. This approach typically leads new runners to increase their mileage far too quickly while simultaneously overemphasizing the weekly long run. Simply put, this style training plan is a recipe for injury and if you do survive it you will most likely still not feel prepared come marathon race day because of the sheer struggle associated with completing long runs in this manner.

A better way

A smarter way to increase mileage is by designing blocks of training that last four weeks at a time.

The first three weeks will have steady mileage. Let us say for example, 20 miles total in each of the first three weeks.

In the first week, the amount of mileage is new to you. Your body needs to adapt to it.

In the second week, your mileage stays steady. Your body is becoming more comfortable with it.

In the third week, your mileage again stays constant. By the end of this week, you should be very comfortable with the mileage.

Now that you are comfortable with the mileage, take a recovery week in the fourth and final week of the block.

Reduce your mileage by approximately 25% in the fourth week to allow yourself the opportunity to absorb the training from the three weeks beforehand and to hedge against injury. In our example, week four would contain just 15 miles of running.

Moving onto the fifth week, you will begin your next block of training. Increase your mileage in the next block by one mile per run completed in each week of the previous block. For example, if you ran five days per week in the previous block, increase your mileage by five miles for the next block. In our example, the increase would be from 20 to 25 miles per week.

Example mileage build

Week 1	Week 2	Week 3	Week 4
25 miles	25 miles	25 miles	19 miles
Week 5	**Week 6**	**Week 7**	**Week 8**
30 miles	30 miles	30 miles	23 miles
Week 9	**Week 10**	**Week 11**	**Week 12**
35 miles	35 miles	35 miles	27 miles
… and so on until your taper period			

How much mileage is too much?

While many passionate amateur athletes are captivated by the 100-mile weeks of professionals, this level of mileage must be given the respect it deserves.

High mileage is only good if you match your mileage with the amount of recovery you give yourself. If these two opposing forces are out of balance, your entire training will come crumbling down.

Professionals can run more because they dedicate the majority of their day to recovery. A pro only runs about two to two-and-a-half hours a day. The other twenty-two hours a day are spent sleeping, strength training, stretching, rehabbing, rehydrating, and eating healthy food.

The passionate adult runner can likely find up to two hours a day to run, but due to the responsibilities of work and family can not match the amount of intentional recovery that a pro puts in. Therefore an amateur runner should not attempt to run as much as a pro or compare their training to that of professionals.

Can you spare the time to sleep 8-10 hours a night and do prehab exercises for 20 minutes a day? If so, that is more than most people. Do what you can while increasing your mileage until you find your highest sustainable amount.

On the flip side, occasionally I come across athletes who I feel are running too many miles per week for their current fitness level or goals. This is typically the case of high-mileage runners who are not posting fast-times in races. In some cases, a reduction in total mileage to allow for more time to recover between runs, and more of an emphasis on faster running can be beneficial. Once this type of runner improves at lower mileage, they can consider adding in more mileage for further improvement.

It is important to remember that while more mileage is better in an ideal world, running more mileage is a stress. Therefore it is only better if you can recover and improve from it. Simply running more miles is not always the answer.

Increasing your mileage from season to season

A general rule of thumb is to not increase your peak mileage more than 10 miles per week from training season to season.

If you successfully run 30 miles per week before your first marathon, in your next season you could train up to 40.

If that goes well, consider going up to 50 in the next season.

Being patient with and intentionally delaying the growth of your mileage over the years will give you a longer and healthier career in distance running. There is no prize awarded for rushing to high-mileage.

4. How To Improve Your Running Form Naturally

Do you run with good form? What is good running form anyway?

In this chapter, we will dive into some of the most frequent questions I get asked as a running coach about improving your running form and dispel some of the myths out there about it.

The good news is that for distance runners your natural running form is probably the best one for you. Forcing changes into your form is in most cases not necessary. Instead, you should naturally improve your running form over time by incorporating training techniques and practices that promote good form.

We all run a little differently

Take a look at any group of runners going along and you will see all different styles of running form. Some athletes run with faster cadence, while others run with less frequent steps. Some have bounding strides and high heel lifts in the back, while others seem more like they are shuffling along, barely lifting their legs off the ground.

Every runner is unique. There is no one correct form that is universal for all athletes. This is because the way you run as an individual is formulated over your entire lifetime of unique movement patterns.

Distance running is one of the simplest of all sports from a technical perspective. Success in running performance relies on aerobic strength, smart tactics, and listening to your body throughout training. Distance running does not rely nearly as much on technical excellence as it does in other sports such as sprint running or swimming. Therefore, discussions on running form for distance runners do not need to be over complicated. Your best running form is typically the one that feels most natural and efficient to you.

Does foot strike matter?

Not as much as some would make you think. The three types of foot strikes are *heel strike, midfoot strike,* and *forefoot strike.*

Heel striking has been villainized since the release of the fantastic book, *Born to Run* by Christopher McDougall. While I highly recommend this book for its entertainment value and great incites into little-known running cultures, the cultural impact this book has had is in many ways unfortunate. *Born to Run* inspired everyday Americans to ditch their normal running shoes in a misguided movement towards minimalist footwear, many runners tried to forcibly change their running form away from heel striking by wearing so-called natural or minimalist footwear. While using minimalist footwear and focusing on how you land with each step can be a very good thing when done appropriately, many runners only found pain and suffering making a dramatic change like this too quickly.

Now years after *Born to Run* was originally published, marketing trends are swinging the other direction. Chunky, high-platform shoes are now the trend. This thick style of shoe is considered faster than minimalist shoes now due to improvements in foam technology. Unfortunately thick shoes do not promote good running form, encourage heel-striking, and should be used in moderation.

Heel striking is the most common way for athletes to run at easy paces. It is natural that as you speed up you shift to a more midfoot strike, and once you reach top speeds you will naturally be forefoot striking.

Take a look at professional runners running in slow motion and you will see that many of them heel strike even at faster speeds. If it is not slowing them down, it most likely will not slow you down either. That said, midfoot striking is considered more biomechanically ideal.

Midfoot striking is considered the ideal way to land for all but the fastest paces. How you land will vary greatly based on not just how fast you are running but also what kind of footwear you are wearing. The best runners vary the styles of footwear they are wearing depending on the goal of the run. Varying footwear ensures you do not land in the same way every single step and therefore distribute the impact forces and conditioning benefits of running more evenly.

Does cadence matter?

In general, when you run *slower* you will have a *slower cadence*, and when you run *faster*, you will have a *faster cadence*.

There is no magic cadence number you want to hit for all running paces or for any specific pace either. There is a myth that 180 steps-per-minute (SPM) is the ideal cadence for all speeds. This is simply not true.

The myth of 180 SPM being the magic number comes from an observation during a professional race in which all of the competitors ran about 180 SPM. The problem is, they were all going at a very fast speed in this race. When these professional runners go out for easy jogs they certainly are not running as quickly as 180 SPM.

Your cadence is also affected by your individual height. Shorter runners have faster cadence typically for the same speed. This is because due to their shorter legs they need to take more steps per minute than a taller, longer-legged runner does to go the same speed.

Do not focus on your specific SPM rate. Instead, focus on running with quick and light steps. Avoid running with long and bounding strides. When your coach tells you to run slow or run easy, you may find it more helpful to think of running lightly. Run like you are running on ice or on shells you do not want to break. Keep your arms moving quickly and your legs will follow. Often these tricks help keep your cadence quick and light when you are tiring in a challenging run.

Should I intentionally change my running form?

In general, no. Do not force change in your movement patterns.

When it comes to adults, your form is the result of your lifetime of growth, movement, and injury. The way you move best is unique to you. Run in the way that feels natural and most efficient to you. That may look very different from others and that is okay.

Purposely changing your form typically results in a decrease in your running efficiency. When you change one aspect of your form for the better you are likely in turn being less efficient in another area. The change you are trying to implement will not be natural to you.

Do caring friends point out odd things about your running style? Those may be worth a closer look, but they also may be totally fine. Remember you are a unique human with a unique anatomy and biomechanics. Many very talented runners have odd form.

Have you repeatedly been injured from running? As a coach, I would assert your running form is likely not the reason for the injury. I believe most injuries come from doing too hard of training or getting inadequate rest, recovery, and nutrition. Look at these factors of your training critically before attempting to make any major changes to your running form.

How to naturally improve your running form

The best way to improve your form as a distance runner is through natural adoption of better form over time. Incorporate the following list of activities into your regular training to better your form.

Run more frequently and with less fatigue - Gradually increase your number of days per week spent running and your total weekly mileage. Your body will naturally find its best running form as you run more frequently.

Perform warm-up drills at least once a week - Practicing warm-up drills which isolate one aspect of running form, such as high-knees and butt kicks, will improve your muscle memory for running with a more efficient form.

Regularly perform speed work and strides - Running faster paces encourages you to run with better, more economical form. Running fast gets you on your midfoot and forefoot as you run. It makes you run with a faster cadence. To run workouts well and push yourself to your limit, you must run with your best form. When you regularly perform speed work, the benefits to your form will extend beyond just the workout. You will incorporate the positive form changes in your everyday easy and long runs as well.

Run hills, especially uphill - Running up and down hills forces you to recruit different muscles and movement patterns on your run, thereby making you a stronger and more resilient runner.

Running uphill specifically helps improve running form because it encourages you to run more on your mid-to-forefoot, drive your arms, and maintain a tall posture.

Incorporate core and upper body strength - Incorporating strength exercises into your weekly routine will give you the muscular endurance to maintain good running form even in the later stages of races and workouts when you are getting tired.

Avoid habits which can hinder your form

Avoid carrying things when you run that will cause an uneven weight distribution on your body and thereby force you to make subtle adjustments to your form.

Unless absolutely necessary, avoid wearing cell-phone holder armbands, running with your phone in your hand, and running with water bottles in your hands. Running backpacks and vests should also be avoided as much as possible. While carrying these things is often necessary, you should leave them at home and try to run unencumbered during fast workouts and long runs.

An exception would be for ultra-runners who plan to carry gear with them during their event. In this case, it is good to train with your gear on.

Form cues to remember

As you tire over a challenging run or race, it is natural for your form to degrade. Often it is those who are best able to keep running with efficient form who are triumphant at the finish line.

Here are cues to remember when you notice your form getting sloppy. These are also good cues to recall when practicing strides and other form drills.

Head – Keep it level and look forward. Relax your face and lower lip. Smile a bit when it gets hard. This will help you breathe better.

Shoulders – Keep them relaxed and over your hips. Your back should be straight up and down, not hunched forward or back. Think to yourself, *"run tall."*

Pelvis – Keep your pelvis upright and in line with your back and shoulders. This will help you lift your knees higher and more powerfully as you run. Again, think *"run tall."* Do not tip your pelvis forward or backward.

Hands – Keep them in loose fists. Pretend you are holding potato chips between your fingers that you do not want to crush.

Arms - Swing them lightly, with your elbows at a 90-degree angle along your sides. Keep your arms relaxed and moving quickly. Your leg speed matches your arm speed. You can often speed up by pumping your arms faster.

Feet - Try to land with your feet under your body. Do not overextend your feet. Think "*quick and light steps*" instead of "*long and bounding strides.*"

5. Warm up to Build Self-Confidence

Importance of the warm-up

Add a dynamic warm-up before every workout and race.

It is obvious before the start of a workout or race who is preparing to truly run hard from the gun and who is not. Design a personalized warm-up consisting of jogging, stretching, drills, and strides. Then be consistent with it. Perform your warm-up routine before every hard run. Not only will this help prepare your body to run fast, your mind will get in the zone too.

By warming up before every hard run, you give yourself the opportunity to clear out bad physical and mental feelings you may be harboring. You take a moment for inward focus and commitment to the task ahead. You build self-confidence in knowing you are doing the little things right that will lead to your success.

Your warm-up should be a ritual. You should perform it without thinking before all hard runs. It should be grounding, calming of pre-race and pre-workout nerves. Whether or not to complete a warm-up is not a choice you should make. The warm-up must be something you just simply do before every workout or race. You will not run your best if you neglect the warm up. Do not think about it, instead just do it.

The goal of the warm-up is to clear out junk and prime your systems for success. It is completely normal to feel bad during your warm-up. This does not mean your workout or race will go poorly. If you feel bad during the warm-up it just means the warm-up is working. Do not be tricked into thinking that just because you feel bad during your warm-up that you are in for a bad performance.

Many of my best workouts and races have come after crummy-feeling warm-ups. Yours will too.

Planning your warm up routine

Start warming up 30 minutes to 60 minutes before your race. The shorter the race, the longer the warm-up needs to be. This is because you need to be more ready to run fast from the start in a shorter race. You need not worry so much about tiring yourself out in the warm-up when preparing for a short race, but for a longer race such as a half or full marathon it is okay to do less.

For example, in preparation for a one-mile race, start jogging up to an hour before the start. Whereas for a marathon, you only need to start 10-20 minutes beforehand or perhaps do no real warm-up at all. For a marathon, it's often best to treat the first few miles of the race as your warm-up.

The exact moves you perform in your warm-up are not as important as simply performing a ritualistic series of moves that make you feel ready to give your best effort.

Do not get so caught up in worrying about what moves are ideal that you give up and fail to consistently perform a sincere warm-up. Any warm-up done consistently is better than no warm-up or an inconsistently done one.

How to warm up, step-by-step

1. Start with a jog of 10 to 20 minutes at a very easy pace

Jogging raises your heart rate and core temperature, thereby increasing the fluidity of your body movements. This will let you run faster and with better form in the workout or race ahead.

Easing into hard running may help prevent injuries caused by unexpected, sudden movements.

Try to relax mentally and physically during your warm-up. Let your mind go quiet and focus on how you are feeling. Stop and notice the nice things around you. Smell the flowers. Enjoy yourself and stay calm.

2. Perform 3 to 10 minutes of dynamic stretches and drills

Performing dynamic stretches and drills will bring your muscles through their full range of motion and prepare them to run fast.

Pick 5 to 10 movements that you like the best and that will engage all areas of the body.

Start with simple movements and finish with more complex movements.

Dynamic movements from simple to complex include: *hip rotations, toe touches, arm circles from the shoulders, high knees, heel pulled to butt, lunges, ground sweeps, hip openers, glute bridges, leg swings, A-Skips, B-Skips, backwards running, sideways skipping, karaoke or grapevine.*

Static stretching is no longer recommended before running. Modern wisdom tells us to instead do dynamic stretches and drills before running. Dynamic movements open up our range of motion without overextending it. Save any static stretching for after your run is complete. Static stretching done before running could potentially damage cold muscles and could overstretch them.

A tight rubber band is more powerful than a loose one. Getting too loose from static stretching before running could actually make you run worse. That said, there is no one-size-fits-all here. Find what works best for you.

A note on barefoot running

Consider doing dynamic warm-up movements with bare-feet or in just socks before workouts or races. A 400 to 800 meter run or walk barefoot makes a great addition to a warm-up. Barefoot cooldown jogs on grass are another great idea. Going barefoot will strengthen your feet, ankles, and lower legs. Most athletes are weak in these areas. Your single-leg balance and running form will also improve by going barefoot. Ease into barefoot activities if you are new to them. It is also worth pointing out that going barefoot as much as possible at home will make you a stronger runner as well.

3. Perform 2 to 4 strides

Run 2 to 4 x 100m strides at your race or workout pace. Give yourself 1 to 2 minutes of rest between each stride to allow for complete recovery. You can not take too much rest here. The goal of these strides is to give you a taste of the pace to come.

By practicing your race pace in the warm-up and you will not be surprised by what race pace feels like when the starting gun goes off. You will not start too fast or too slow.

4. Final actions and go time

End your last stride 5 to 10 minutes before the start of the race. This will let you recover fully before the start. If you are warming up for a workout, you can just jump right into it once you feel ready.

About 10 minutes before the start of a race, use the bathroom one last time, then go to the corral and seed yourself. If the bathroom lines are long, you may need to do some warming up while waiting in line.

A few minutes before the start, take off any extra layers you are wearing and leave them at the start with a friend or in a drop bag.

In the corral, keep warm with some more dynamic movements. At this point you should feel ready to run at race pace, so just stay warm however works best for you. For a race 10K and shorter, you'll ideally be sweating slightly before the start. For races longer than 10K, you can continue to warm up in the first mile or two of the race.

If it is cold, avoid ending your warm-up prematurely and letting yourself cool down before the start.

If it is hot, make sure you do not get so hot during your warm-up your performance will be compromised. While minor sweating before a race is good, if you are sweating profusely before a race that is a bad sign.

When the race starts, remember the first mile of any distance race will always feel very easy. It is supposed to. Stay calm and relaxed. Do not push the pace faster in the beginning. Most likely you'll need to intentionally slow yourself down at the start so you can save your energy for the middle and end.

Special considerations for warming up before a marathon race

Because simply running the 26.2 mile distance is a challenge for all but the most elite runners, consider performing a significantly shorter warmup before a marathon race. Instead of jogging for 10 to 20 minutes before a marathon, you can treat the first mile or two of the marathon as your warm-up.

Treating the first few miles of the marathon as your warm up will effectively shorten the distance you need to cover during the day and prevent you from starting too fast. Before a marathon race, a few minutes of walking or very light jogging combined with easy dynamic stretches in the starting corral should be enough.

Practice makes perfect

When you first start practicing your warm-up, you may feel goofy and perhaps even a little embarrassed. Do not worry, this feeling will go away and be replaced with confidence as you realize your ritual is leading you to success.

Before your next race, look at those warming up around you. You will almost certainly see all the fast-looking people warming up hard. If you want to be fast, you need to warm up hard too. It is important to practice before race day and be comfortable with your warm-up. You will see a lot of people on race day performing silly movements they have never practiced before. Trying some new stretch or drill on race day is just a bad idea. You do not want to tweak anything right before showtime.

6. Fueling Your Best Marathon

When preparing for a marathon, your physical training is obviously important — racking up the miles, crushing interval workouts, and spending hours on your feet — but you also need to practice your nutrition. Fueling correctly on the run is a crucial part of getting through 26.2 miles feeling strong. Creating a personalized marathon fueling plan is essential. Practicing your plan and ensuring it works for you during long runs in training is even more important. Successful fueling can make the difference between just barely finishing a marathon or setting a new PR while feeling great from start to finish.

How important is it to fuel on your run?

Fueling on the run becomes very important during runs that are longer than 60 minutes. After running for 60 to 90 minutes, your body will start to run low on glycogen - your body's carbohydrate stores. Glycogen is the fuel source in your body that is the limiting factor to fast endurance exercise. When you run low on glycogen, you physically can not keep up the intensity and pace of your run.

How often should you eat during a marathon?

How much you personally need for optimal performance is a very individual thing. The aim of fueling on the run is to maintain blood sugar levels (glycogen), and how often you need to fuel to achieve this will depend on your intensity (pace), length of run, and your body composition. While fueling every 30 to 45 minutes will probably suit most runners, there are no hard and fast rules.

As a starting point, most marathoners should start fueling 30 to 45 minutes into the race, and then take in additional fuel every 30 minutes thereafter. For 3:00 hour marathoners and faster, you may want to fuel more frequently, perhaps every twenty minutes. This is because the faster you run, the more rapidly you deplete your internal energy stores.

The time-frames given here are starting points only. Every athlete is different and you should experiment with fueling during your long runs to determine what is optimal for you. When in doubt, err on the side of fueling more frequently. Most marathoners do not consume enough fuel during their workouts, long runs, or races for optimal performance.

Do you need energy gels for a marathon?

Not everyone loves gels, and you definitely do not *need* them to fuel your marathon. However, they can be very useful when it comes to running 26.2 miles. I have tried many different energy gels over the years and what works for me may not work for you. Everyone reacts differently to gels. Some love them, some hate them. Nowadays there are many styles and flavors of energy gels and gel-alternatives on the market. Many runners prefer to get most of their caloric needs from sports drinks during the marathon. Some like to use energy chews. Others prefer natural fuels like dates or maple syrup. Experiment to find out what works best for you.

Aim to take in 200 to 400 calories per hour, remembering how much is best for you depends on a number of factors that you must test in training.

Is caffeine good for long-distance running?

The golden rule with caffeine is to ensure you have tried it during training. Caffeine is a stimulant and can help improve your energy levels, especially during those last few miles of the marathon. Some athletes react negatively to caffeine, so test how you react to it before your next important race. Let your experience be your guide. If you are not up for a coffee or espresso shot pre-workout, there are caffeinated gels, gums, or even pills available these days.

The two most popular ways of taking caffeine for a marathon involve either alternating between un-caffeinated and caffeinated gels throughout the race, or saving the caffeinated gels for the final third of the race when the going typically gets tough. Waiting to take caffeine until the end of the race may help keep you sharp after several hours on the run. But staying caffeinated throughout may hedge against hitting the wall in the first place. If you plan to take caffeine during a marathon, you should experiment with the different approaches during your long runs to find out which method works best for you.

Rules for marathon fueling

1. Do not try anything new on race day

Do not try anything on race day that you have not practiced during training. Test different fuel options, amounts, and timings during your long runs and workouts. Take note of what works for you and what does not. Once you develop a nutrition plan that works for you, commit to it and bring it to the starting line with you.

2. Mid-run fueling is a must

Perhaps you got by on a few long runs without fueling, but over the course of 26.2 miles, you need to fuel in order to run your fastest. It is better to have a little extra nutrition stowed away than to not have enough and bonk at mile 18 or 20. Glycogen is the energy source in your body that lets you run fast and it will deplete fully after about 90 minutes of running if you do not actively refuel yourself. Therefore to run a marathon to your full potential, you *must* fuel.

3. Listen to your body

While you are practicing your fueling strategy during long runs, pay attention to how you feel toward the end of the run and after you finish. If you finish feeling good, you likely have a great nutrition plan in place. But if you feel totally wiped out, try adding 15 grams of carbs per hour to your fueling plan. If you finish feeling energized but with GI distress, you probably ate too much, did not drink enough water, or need to experiment with other fuel sources.

4. Pre-marathon meals

Your pre-race meals are critical for success. For the final two to three meals before your race, choose high-carb, moderate-protein, and low-fat and fiber options. The meals should be easily digestible for you. Avoid new foods or heavily spiced dishes. Favorites in the Knighton household include a pasta dinner with plenty of water at night, followed by a bagel topped with a scoop of peanut butter, a banana, and black coffee for breakfast.

5. Fueling does not stop at the finish line

To jumpstart recovery after a race, workout, or long run, consume approximately 50 grams of carbohydrates within 30 minutes of finishing the activity. A bit of protein is helpful too but remember that carbs are the primary source of fuel for runners. A 4-to-1 ratio of carbs-to-protein is a good rule of thumb for refueling after a hard activity. Immediately drink water as well since you are likely a bit dehydrated too. If you will be finishing your exercise away from home, be sure to bring a snack and water bottle with you so that you can begin refueling immediately after completing your activity.

The Six Phases of
Marathon Training

There are six phases of marathon training. In each phase, place your focus on one specific aspect of training. This phased approach allows you to improve significantly in one area before moving on to the next. Following these six phases in order will allow you to build up the physical strength and mental confidence to run faster at your next marathon.

Phase 1 - Base Building

Always lay the foundation first

Whether you are a brand new runner or a veteran returning from a break, all athletes should start their training at the foundational level.

The base building phase is the time to establish your weekly framework of running. Increase the frequency and distance of your runs during this phase. Get into a routine that is comfortable for you and that you can expand upon in the more demanding phases of training ahead.

Virtually all of your running in the base building phase should be done at comfortable effort levels. Keep your runs easy. If you participate in any faster workouts during this phase they should be kept light, short, and run them by effort only, not for time.

Include a base building phase at the beginning of every marathon-training season. By laying a strong foundation at the beginning of every training cycle, you set yourself up for the best probability of success.

Why is base building important?

Physical transformations

During this phase, you are literally rebuilding your body from the inside out. Consistent easy running early in your training season does the following:

- Your heart is strengthened, allowing for more blood flow per beat and a slower heart rate.
- You increase the number, size, and distribution of mitochondria in your muscle cells, allowing for more energy generation when running.
- You activate more capillaries over time, thereby providing more oxygen to your running muscles.
- Your muscles get better at conserving your limited glycogen (carbohydrate fuel) and instead start using more stored fat for energy. Fat-based energy stores are essentially unlimited, no matter how lean of an athlete you are.
- Your bones, muscles, and tendons stress and react to the running and recreate themselves stronger.

All these benefits come from low intensity running. The changes may not display outwardly for others to see, but your body is changing, building, and strengthening on the inside.

Injury prevention

By base building, you are building a body that is more resilient to injury.

Anywhere from 65% to 80% of runners develop injuries over the course of a year. These injuries are primarily due to poor decisions made in training.

Spending a long time in the base building phase allows your muscles, tendons, and bones to stress and adapt to running, thereby becoming stronger over time. By building a strong base, you prepare yourself for the harder work to come in the later phases of marathon training.

High-intensity intervals, tempo runs, and marathon-pace running is very important to complete if you want to perform your best, but these runs are the fastest way to injury for a runner who has not laid a sufficient base.

Simply put, sufficient base building at the start of each season is an insurance plan against getting sidelined. Do not fast forward it.

An opportunity to increase your weekly mileage

During the base building phase, you are able to more safely increase your weekly mileage to higher levels before launching into hard workouts. Running higher mileage is almost always better for distance runners.

How do you build mileage, especially if you think you are prone to injury or not well suited to high mileage? The answer lies in a long base phase consisting of easy running and patiently growing your mileage over time.

What holds most runners back is doing work that is too hard, too often. Patience and wise guidance will let any runner build a strong base. It is safer to only add in one stress at a time to your training. This could be more mileage or more speed. By increasing your mileage during the base building phase, you can do so without simultaneously needing to focus on faster running intensity.

How to build your base

Duration

Treat yourself to a month or more of mostly easy running before beginning any structured workouts. Be patient and recall that during this phase you are giving yourself time to strengthen your body so it can handle the harder training to come.

Frequency

Build the habit of regular running during the base phase. Increase your number of running days to at least five days a week. Four days a week should be considered the minimum for any runner looking to improve their fitness. To do your best in the marathon, five to seven days of running per week will be necessary for most athletes. Older athletes or those with ongoing injuries may want to replace some of these days with non-impact cardio-based cross-training.

Volume

Build your weekly mileage during the base phase without the added stress of fast workouts or excessively long runs. Increase your mileage patiently over time. Only move to a higher mileage when you are 100% confident your body and mind has adapted to the stress of your current workload.

Variety

After several weeks of purely easy running, consider adding strides or light effort-based workouts for variety. These will help prepare you for the more challenging workouts to come.

The base phase is a great time to explore new running routes. Ideally you'll have a different route to run for each day of the week. If you include both flat and hilly roads and trails in your weekly runs you will be best prepared for whatever running throws at you. While your effort level should stay comfortable for almost all of your running in the base phase, no two runs are the same if your runs travel over different routes, on different days, during different weather. Variety is a good thing. Seek it out during base training.

Phase 2 - Speed Development

What is speed development running?

Speed development running is running performed at a pace significantly faster than your marathon goal race pace. While any mileage covered faster than marathon pace can be considered speed work, speed development happens most rapidly at speeds two to three notches faster than goal pace.

For marathoners, speed work typically consists of runs performed at 5K to 10K race pace for durations of one to five minutes.

Why focus on speed development?

Each phase of marathon training focuses on building one aspect of your skillset. After the base building phase, you will feel strong, resilient, and eager for faster running. The speed development phase comes second to capitalize on the foundation you have built over the previous phase.

By regularly running at racing speeds two to three notches faster than your goal marathon pace, you will rapidly develop your aerobic strength and top-end speed. Your goal marathon pace will feel significantly easier after you have run workouts at a much faster pace over four to six weeks.

During the speed development phase, place the most emphasis on your weekly speed workout. This focus will allow you to gain the greatest physiological benefit from the work while giving you the confidence you need to run your marathon at your goal race pace.

When you extend the length of your long runs in the next phase, the race-specific quality phase, you will already be fast enough to comfortably handle your goal marathon pace. Because you are fast enough already, you can then simply focus on covering the distance of the runs themselves, rather than having to get faster while simultaneously going further.

Simply put, the purpose of this phase is to *get fast before you have to go far.*

How much speedwork should be done?

Perform one speed-development workout each week for a period of four to six weeks.

Two fast miles per week is sufficient for a runner totaling 30 miles per week.

Three fast miles per week is sufficient for a runner totaling 40+ miles per week.

Four to five fast miles per week can be done on occasion and with an abundance of caution by high mileage runners covering 60+ miles per week.

When in doubt, less is more with speed work. Focus on quality over quantity.

Supplement your speed work by adding in 4 to 8 x 100m strides at the end of most of your easy runs. These strides should be run at about a 9 out of 10 intensity (or around one-mile race pace) and should have full recoveries between them.

Types of speed development workouts

Speed development for marathoners can be performed as fartleks, track workouts, or road workouts. Choose your favorite style of workout that matches your strengths and will keep you engaged throughout the phase. Alternatively, it is possible to mix the three types of workouts together during this phase.

Fartlek Speed Series

Progress through this series over your speed development phase.

Run the fast minutes at your current 5K to 10K race effort level. The effort should feel hard. Focus on running fast but relaxed. Recover with jogging slow enough to maintain consistency over the duration of the workout.

Fartleks can be run on any terrain and are great when training for hilly races. The beauty of fartleks is they are purely effort based. There are no specific paces to hit. You can ignore the pace on your watch and get in tune with your body during these runs. Fartleks are fun and feel more like playing than like a serious workout.

Week 1 – 1:00 FAST / 1:00 JOG
Week 2 – 2:00 FAST / 1:00 - 2:00 JOG
Week 3 – 3:00 FAST / 2:00 - 3:00 JOG
Week 4 – 4:00 FAST / 3:00 – 4:00 JOG
Week 5 – 5:00 FAST / 4:00 – 5:00 JOG

Track Speed Series

Perform one of these workouts each week, progressing through the series.

Run the fast intervals at your current 5K to 10K race pace. Focus on running fast but relaxed. Recover with jogging slow enough to maintain consistency over the duration of the workout.

The track series is perfect for the marathoner training for a flat race. Run the first couple intervals to the time on your watch, but then try to run by effort-level to develop an innate sense of what your target pace feels like.

Week 1 – 400M FAST / 400M JOG
Week 2 – 600M FAST / 400M JOG
Week 3 – 800M FAST / 400M JOG
Week 4 – 1000M FAST / 400M JOG
Week 5 – 1200M FAST / 400M JOG

Road Speed Series

Perform one of these workouts each week, progressing through the series.

Run at your current 5K to 10K race pace. The effort should feel hard. Focus on running fast but relaxed. Recover with jogging slow enough to maintain consistency over the duration of the workout.

Run the road series on any safe flat road or running path.

Week 1 – 0.25 MILE FAST / 0.25 MILE JOG
Week 2 – 0.50 MILE FAST / 0.25 MILE JOG
Week 3 – 0.75 MILE FAST / 0.25 MILE JOG
Week 4 – 1.0 MILE FAST / 0.50 MILE JOG
Week 5 – Repeat your favorite workout from above

After four to six weeks of being speed-focused, you will be feeling much faster than at the start of training and will be ready to take on your goal marathon pace in long runs.

Phase 3 - Race-Specific Quality

What is race-specific running?

Race-specific running is running that best prepares you for the specific demands of your race. To be successful at the marathon, you must develop not only a strong aerobic engine but also build an incredibly resilient skeletal-muscular system that can carry you for 26.2 miles at top speed.

Marathon-specific training includes significant amounts of miles done in environments similar to that you will experience on race day. Conditions you should practice on include: flat vs. hilly routes, trying to match the weather, time of day, etc.

The race-specific quality phase combines long runs with workouts run at or near your goal marathon pace. Spending six to twelve weeks in this phase will condition your body to run your goal pace for 26.2 miles.

Why focus on race-specific training?

Most marathoners simply do not have enough strength and resiliency in their bodies to go the full length of the marathon at the top speed their aerobic engine will allow.

Shorter events like 5K to Half Marathon rely heavily on your aerobic engine and natural talent, but in the marathon it is impossible to succeed without putting in race-specific work.

The marathon is a battle of attrition for most athletes. Your limiting factor is not how fast your legs can move or how fast you can process oxygen like in the shorter events. In the marathon, your limiting factor is most likely your resilience to sheer muscular fatigue and breakdown.

I speak from experience, having run multiple marathons at what I thought was an extremely comfortable effort, only to find my legs absolutely shattered by mile 20. This caused me to not just gradually slow down, as I would in a shorter race, but instead forced me to walk despite my best efforts to continue running.

In the race-specific quality phase of training, you will focus on building your physical resilience so you can go the distance at your goal pace.

What does race-specific training look like?

Perform two race-specific workouts each week for a period of six to twelve weeks.

The first weekly workout should be slightly faster than goal marathon pace. It serves to make your goal pace feel more comfortable.

The second weekly workout can be either a midweek tempo at or faster than marathon pace, or can be a workout done as part of your long run.

Choosing your marathon pace

Your marathon pace is best estimated using a race conversion calculator. Plug in your finish time from a half marathon or 10K to get an approximation of what you could expect to run over a full marathon if properly trained.

Note that these calculators will be more accurate if you plug in a longer race like a half marathon, rather than a shorter race like a 5K.

A rougher way to estimate your marathon time is to take your most recent half marathon finish time, double it and then add ten minutes.

It is smart to err on the side of caution when using calculators to predict your marathon pace. The physical demands of the marathon are more like that of an ultra marathon than they are like a half marathon for most runners. Most athletes will run slower at the marathon than these calculators predict because while the athlete likely has the speed they need to run the predicted time, they lack the physical endurance needed to cover 26.2 miles at the predicted pace without breakdown.

Marathon-Specific Speed Work

Perform 3 to 6 miles per week of running slightly faster than your goal marathon pace.

If you run *30 miles per week*, run 3 miles fast.

If you run *40 miles per week*, run 4 miles fast.

If you run *50 miles per week*, run 5 miles fast.

If you run *60+ miles per week*, run 6 miles fast.

These miles can be covered in intervals, fartleks, or steady tempo runs.

Your speed for this faster-than-marathon-pace running could be just 10 seconds per mile faster than goal marathon pace. If you want slightly faster, it could be half marathon pace to lactate threshold tempo pace.

Adjust the pace and duration of recovery between intervals accordingly. The faster you go in your intervals, the slower your recovery jogs should be. A good rule of thumb is to apply a 5:1 to 3:1 work-rest ratio to this style of run.

Remember to never turn training into a race.

When in doubt, less is more with speed work. Focus on quality over quantity.

Marathon-Specific Steady Pace Work

The second weekly workout should be a midweek tempo run at slightly faster than marathon pace, a fartlek hovering around marathon pace, a strong long run approaching marathon pace, or a long run with goal marathon pace built in.

Run your marathon-specific steady pace workouts on terrain similar to what you will experience on your marathon course at least every other week.

Grow the distance of your long run and duration of faster running over the course of your training, so that before the taper you can comfortably cover at least 10 miles at goal marathon pace in a 16 to 20-mile long run.

Try to avoid putting more than 30-40% of your total weekly mileage into a single long run. Consistency across the week is more valuable and safer than over-emphasizing long runs. Lower mileage runners need not exceed 16 mile long runs.

Types of Marathon Specific Workouts

Marathon specific workouts are best done on the types of terrain you expect to run on during your goal race. If you are training for a flat race, do your pace-based workouts on a flat course. If you are training for a hilly race, make sure you do at least half of your workouts on a hilly course.

The track may be used for the speed workouts during this phase, but you may find the road, a bike path, or trail more enjoyable for long intervals.

Choose the types of workouts that you most enjoy and play to your strengths. Alternatively, choose to run workouts that improve upon your weaknesses.

Marathon-Specific Speed Series

Progress through a series such as the one below during your marathon race-specific quality phase. Adjust the total number of intervals covered to be appropriate for your weekly mileage.

Run at 10 seconds per mile faster than goal marathon pace or up to your lactate threshold effort level. These workouts are about building strength and confidence over long intervals run faster than marathon pace.

You may find these workouts are not that challenging, especially if you opt to run them between marathon and half marathon pace. That is okay. They are aerobic workouts meant to make you stronger physically for the marathon. You do not need to run faster to get the desired effect. Stay controlled. If you feel as though your goal marathon pace is still a bit too fast, consider running these intervals faster, closer to your lactate threshold, to get more of a speed-endurance stimulus.

Recover with easy running or jogging slow enough to maintain consistency over the duration of the workout.

Week 1 – 6 x 1 mile w/ 0.25 mile easy
Week 2 – 4 x 1.5 mile w/ 0.5 mile easy

Week 3 – 3 x 2 mile w/ 0.5 mile easy

Week 4 – 2 x 3 mile w/ 1.0 mile easy

Week 5 – 10 x 1000M w/ 200M jog

Week 6 – 2 x 3 mile w/ 1.0 mile easy

Week 7 – 3 x 2 mile w/ 0.5 mile easy

Week 8 – 6 x 1 mile w/ 0.25 mile easy

Marathon-Specific Long Runs

Being fast enough is just one piece of the marathon puzzle. To be successful in the marathon, you also need to be able to cover the full distance at your goal pace. To prepare your body for this, you need to perform three types of long runs over varying types of terrain. Run on the type of terrain your race will be on, such as a flat vs. hilly course, at least every other week in your long run.

Long Run Type 1 – Long Slow Distance

If you are new to the marathon, this will be your most important type of long run. It does not matter your speed if you can not cover the distance. In this long run your only goal is to simply cover the distance. This long run is mostly about improving your aerobic system and conditioning your skeletal-muscular system to handle the impacts of running for hours on end. Cover this run at a comfortable, easy pace.

Work up to being able to run for 2 to 2.5 hours comfortably on your long run each week. Runs over 2.5 hours are very hard on our bodies and take longer to recover from. Any run over 2.5 hours should be taken seriously and given the respect it deserves in terms of post-run recovery. Because of this, most marathoners should not run longer than 3 hours in their training, even if they are working towards a marathon goal in the 3:30 to 5:00+ range.

If you perform consistent long runs in the 2 to 2.5 hour range, you will get in better marathon shape than if you try to perform runs longer than 2.5+ hours.

Long Run Type 2 – Strong Steady Effort (i.e., Marathon Pace + ~30 seconds per mile or 95% of Goal Marathon Pace)

The second type of marathon long run you may want to incorporate into your training is the strong and steady long run at a pace close to but slightly slower than goal marathon pace.

By running about 30 seconds per mile slower than marathon pace (or around 95% of your goal pace), you get most of the physical benefits of running marathon pace but at a significantly easier effort. While in heavy training it may be hard to hold 10 miles at marathon pace, but it can feel fairly easy to hold significantly more miles around 30 seconds per mile slower than marathon pace.

This pace is not easy like the long slow distance run described above. It is more of a moderate pace. Towards the end of the run, the pace will likely start to feel quite hard. Think of it as the fastest end of your easy-pace spectrum. You feel good and like you are working, but it is sustainable. This strong, feel-good pace often gives the fabled runner's high.

When coaches talk about athletes doing their everyday easy runs too hard, it is typically running done in this MP+30 pace range. This pace is too fast to be truly easy or restorative, but not fast enough to be your actual marathon pace or target any of the higher intensity physiological thresholds. Generally on an easy day it is preferable to instead run slower, but this is not necessarily true on the long run. While you want to avoid this easy-to-moderate running intensity most of the time, this intensity is great for increasing your aerobic capacity and endurance on long runs.

This type of long run may be more applicable to faster marathoners who find their goal marathon pace more of a challenge to hold in training. Faster marathoners have a marathon goal pace that is a higher relative intensity than slower marathoners, so they are more challenged to reach it during training.

Runners who have little difficulty reaching their marathon pace and instead need to work on physical endurance to cover 26.2 miles without breaking down may be better suited performing the following type of long run – the marathon pace run.

Long Run Type 3 – The Marathon Pace Long Run

The marathon pace long run is arguably the best training for an athlete preparing to run the marathon at a target pace. It is certainly the most specific type of training you can do.

Perform a marathon pace long run or mid-week tempo at marathon pace at least every other week in training. Increase the duration you run at marathon pace from just a few miles at the start of training all the way up to 10 or more in the final weeks tapering down.

If you can run 10 to 16 miles at your goal marathon pace in training, you will be able to go the full distance on race day. It is not advised to run more than 14 to 16 miles at marathon race pace in training, because it is potentially too damaging to the body when under a heavy training-load fatigue. If you can cover this distance at your goal marathon pace in training, then most likely your marathon goal pace is easier than it needs to be.

Running more than 14 to 16 miles at marathon pace in training risks injury and sabotaging your training. Hard long runs require a lot of recovery. Never do a long run so demanding that it takes away from your best possible race. Do not overemphasize the importance of the long run.

Examples of Marathon-Specific Long Runs

Mid-week tempo – 2 miles easy, 6 miles at marathon pace, 2 miles cooldown. *Paired with Weekend Long Run* – Long Slow Distance for 16 miles.

Mid-week fartlek – 2 miles warm up, 20 x 1:00 faster than MP, 1:00 slower than MP, 2 miles cool down. *Paired with Weekend Long Run* – 16 miles total, with final 10 at MP+30's per mile.

Weekend Long Run – 3 miles easy, 10 miles at marathon pace, 3 miles cooldown.

Weekend Long Run – 8 miles easy to steady, 10 miles at marathon pace, 2 miles cooldown.

Phase 4 - Tapering for Peak Performance

What is a taper?

The taper is the name given to the period 10 to 21 days before your season's goal marathon. During the taper, you should intentionally run less to allow yourself the opportunity to freshen up before race day. When done correctly, tapering will cause you to reach your peak level of fitness for a very short window of time. Your goal marathon is then run during this peak fitness window before any detraining effect from the reduction in mileage occurs.

Why taper before an important race?

Tapering for the marathon is essential to achieve optimal performance on race day.

Marathon training works on the principle of *cumulative fatigue.*

Cumulative fatigue is the idea that throughout marathon training, you are never fully rested between runs. Each run and workout piles on additional stress which is managed but never relieved over the course of training. Every workout, every long run, and every recovery run is done on tired legs and is often started with depleted glycogen stores.

The taper allows you to fully relieve the weight of cumulative fatigue and completely top up your energy stores before race day. By reducing your daily mileage in the lead-up to your marathon, the fitness you have developed over the past several months can finally emerge and present itself for a peak performance on race day.

Athletes who do not taper after months of diligent training will likely start their marathon fatigued and low on energy.

What does the taper look like?

The optimal makeup of the taper for each athlete is learned only through experience. Some athletes benefit from a longer taper, while others feel stale when reducing their mileage for too long and will therefore require a shorter taper.

As a starting point, a ten-day taper can be used for most athletes. The reason for a ten-day taper is that it takes approximately ten days for the benefits of any workout to manifest into fitness gains within you. Any workout or long run completed within ten days of a key race is more likely to tire you out than to benefit you physically for race day. Runs performed in the taper period are for building mental confidence and developing your sense of freshness only.

Starting ten days before your goal race, reduce the mileage of all of your runs by 50% per run. For example, if you typically run eight miles on Wednesdays, you should run just four miles on Wednesdays in the taper. Keep the same frequency to your runs and complete them at the same intensity as normal. If you perform double runs, consider eliminating your shorter recovery doubles during the taper.

While no hard workouts should be done within the taper period, all running should be performed at normal training paces. Any speed work done within this period should be kept short so as to not fatigue you.

If based upon your personal experience, a ten-day taper was either too long or too short for your liking, you can modify it in your next season's taper period. Talk to your coach about how you can improve your taper next season or make detailed notes about your taper experience if you are self-coached.

It is common to see professional athletes running 100+ miles per week taper gradually over the course of three to four weeks. But for the typical adult marathoner running 30 to 70 miles per week, more than 10 to 14 days of tapering is likely excessive. If your taper is too long it will result in a detraining effect because of your reduction in mileage.

On the flip side, if an athlete has not completed sufficient training before their marathon and is not feeling a lot of day-to-day fatigue, they may be served best either with no taper at all or a very short half-week taper. This will allow the underprepared athlete more time to train before their race.

Examples of marathon taper long runs and workouts

While no hard or long workouts should be completed during the taper phase, it is helpful to complete light workouts during this phase to maintain consistency and keep in touch with race pace.

An example long run during the taper phase, which would occur one week before race day, is 90-minutes at a steady pace (*e.g., ~30 seconds per mile slower than marathon pace*) on a flat route. For athletes who trained at lower mileage, 90-minutes may be too long for them, in which case they could run 50% of the distance of their previous full-length long run.

An example workout during the taper phase is *2 miles easy, 2 miles @ marathon pace, 2 miles easy.* This race-week workout allows the athlete to perform a dress rehearsal of race day early in the week before their goal marathon without tiring them out.

Considerations during the marathon taper

During the taper, pay extra attention to your nutrition, hydration, and quality of sleep. Now is the time to top off your energy stores that have been depleted during training.

Consider eating more carb-rich foods during the taper. Reduce or eliminate alcohol, caffeine, and other substances that can impact your sleep. Drink lots of water and pay attention to electrolyte consumption in the build-up to race day.

Start preparing logistically for race day. Figure out your race day logistics well in advance, if possible, so you do not need to scramble the day before.

Prepare mentally for race day as well. Write down your goals on a piece of paper. Look at them every single day between now and race day. Recite to yourself what you are going to accomplish.

Tell yourself, *"I will accomplish my goal to..."* Do this every day until you are 100% confident in your ability. Then continue this practice through race day.

Trust your training and believe in yourself. You have done the training and now it is time to let the magic of the taper take effect. You have been tired throughout marathon training, but now you are letting that go.

You will be prepared to fly come race day.

Phase 5 – Race Day Performance

After a successful training season and a restful taper, your marathon will mostly run itself. Excellence on race day simply comes down to proper planning, believing in yourself, believing in your training, and running with smart tactics.

How To Plan The Night Before A Race

The Six P's: Proper Preparation Prevents Piss–Poor Performance

After months of hard work, the night before race day has finally arrived. Knowing how to plan the night before a race will ensure you have a successful and stress-free race morning.

Print out or write down all important race details, lay out the clothing and gear you will need for the race, make a detailed schedule for the morning, and then go to bed early.

This plan will serve you well no matter what race distance you are running.

1. Review important race and travel details

Read the latest emails from the race organizer

They may contain important last-minute changes. Check the race website for any last-minute details.

Check the hourly weather for the race

Will it be hot, cold, or mild? Sunny or overcast? Windy or calm? Use this information to inform your clothing choices and race strategy. If it will be a warm race, you should adjust your goal pace using an online pace calculator.

Do not waste your time or mental energy checking the weather several days in advance! It is okay to check once during the week before, but remember that weather can and will change. Obsessing over this will only add stress. Remember that the weather, no matter if it is hot or cold, rain or shine, will affect *all* runners. Embrace the weather for what it is and appreciate the opportunity to do your best on the course with the weather of the day.

Confirm how you will get to the event

If driving, review and write down the directions. Sometimes GPS does not work.

Where can you park? Where is bib pickup? Where is the start line?

Do you need to allow for extra time for bathroom pit stops or traffic enroute to the race? Give yourself ample time to get there. It is better to be very early than even a little bit late.

2. Lay out your clothing and pack a gear bag

Based on the weather, lay out the clothing, shoes, fuel, and accessories you will race with. You want to look sharp on race day. There is truth in the saying, *"look good, feel good, run good."*

Unless it is a hot summer race, lay out a warm-up kit consisting of a long-sleeve top, athletic pants, warm hat, light jacket, buff, and gloves.

When you wake up in the morning, get your racing kit on right away. Make sure to put your warm-up kit on top of it. You should travel to the race wearing these clothes so you can save time by not having to change when you get to the event.

Pack a gear bag with body lubricant, your racing shoes, a water bottle, a pre-race snack or energy gel, a post-race snack or meal, spare socks (in case yours get wet before the race), and any other essentials.

For your gear bag, use a backpack or duffle bag big enough to hold your warm-up clothes and training shoes when you strip them down pre-race. You can stash this bag in the gear-check (if there is one), with a friend, in your vehicle, or in a discrete spot before the race starts.

3. Write down your schedule for the morning

Verify when the race *starts* and then work backward.

Give yourself some buffer for each step. Things always take longer than expected. There is no need to rush.

Here is an example: If the race starts at 8:00am then you know you need to be in the starting corral at ~7:50am (or earlier for a major marathon or large race). Therefore you need to start your warmup by 7:00am. This means you need to pick up your bib at 6:45am. And so you need to get to the parking location at 6:30am. You need to leave your house at 5:30am, and thus you need to wake up at 4:30am.

In this case, your written-down schedule would be:

4:30am – *ALARM CLOCK*

5:30am – *LEAVE HOME*

6:30am – *ARRIVE AT RACE PARKING*

6:45am – *BIB PICKUP*

7:00am – *START WARMUP*

7:50am – *LINE UP AT START*

8:00am – *RACE START*

4. Go to bed early

Rest assured, you have done all you can to prepare. Just like on Christmas Eve, the sooner you go to bed the sooner the big day will come.

Occasionally athletes will struggle to sleep well the night before an important race. If this happens to you, do not worry. If you have been practicing good habits and getting plenty of sleep in the week leading up to race day, then one poor night's sleep will not affect how well you do.

Simply try your best to sleep well the night before and then have a great race. Preparation makes all the difference.

Simple Mental Strategy for Racing – The Three C's

Three C's... Comfortable, Confident, Compete

Running is physical, but success is mental. The difference between finishing a race strong and proud versus crumbling at the end rarely comes down to physical limitations, but instead lies in your mental game.

It is rare and arguably downright impossible to push yourself to your absolute limit in a race, so having a mental approach to racing and giving it equal weight to your physical preparation is of utmost importance.

My favorite mental strategy for most distance running events is to break the race down into three parts. In each part, your mental energy should be spent focusing on *just one word*: Comfortable, Confident, or Compete.

Distance	5K	10K	13.1M	26.2M
Comfortable	Mile 1	Miles 1 - 2	Miles 1 - 5	Miles 1 - 10
Confident	Mile 2	Miles 3 - 4	Miles 6 - 10	Miles 11 - 20
Compete	Mile 3	Miles 5 - 6.2	Miles 10 - 13.1	Miles 20 - 26.2

Suggestions for how to break down common racing distances.

Part One – Comfortable

Distance races are never won in their first third, but this is where they are most commonly lost. Starting line energy and excitement tricks most runners into starting way too hard and fast. Your goals at the start of any race should be to 1) get into the right position in the field and 2) stay comfortable.

Comfortable, comfortable... comfortable

The first third should feel easy. You will be running race pace, but it will not even feel like it. The hard part will come. Do not be tricked by the ease of the early race and run too fast. Run according to plan. Think, *"comfortable, comfortable, comfortable."*

Part Two – Confident

The mid-race. This is where you just need to settle in and stay the course. This middle section could be as short as five minutes in a 5K, or over an hour in a marathon. The key is to get through it and reach the final part of the race feeling strong.

The middle of the race is where you gain confidence.

You are approaching half-way now... and now you are over half-way.

This is distance running. It is simple. Just keep turning over your legs. How much further now? Can you hold this pace? You have come this far already, so of course you can. Gain confidence. You have done this before in training. Think, *"confident, confident, confident."*

If any negative thought comes into your mind, counter it with the positive affirmation, *"I will do this."*

Part Three – Compete

The final stretch. This is where the racing starts. With just one mile to go in the 5K or 6.2 miles left in the marathon, your goal in any distance race is to get to the final stretch feeling strong. You can always make up time in the final third of a race if the opening two parts were a little conservative.

Now that you have stayed comfortable in the first third of the race and gained confidence in the second third, it is time to fly towards the finish line.

This is where you start to compete. The final third of the race is what separates success from failure. It is a mental game. If you made it this far with comfort and confidence, it will not be physical fatigue that threatens your race, it will be mental. But you will remain strong.

Dig in. Why are you doing this race? What are you trying to prove? Who and what are you running for? You love racing. It is why you are here. So give it 100%. It will be hard, but a few moments of pain are worth it for the everlasting satisfaction you will have in your success.

This is what the training was for. All those weeks and months of hard workouts come down to this final stretch of your race. Do not give up. Stay confident. Forget comfort. Go all out!

Finish your race running hard to the end. High-five and congratulate your competition. Enjoy your success.

Phase 6 – Post-Race Recovery

After your goal race, take planned time off and truly shut down your season.

As competitive runners seeking personal bests, we are constantly looking for ways to improve. One easy way to get better in running that athletes often overlook and undervalue is to take a significant break after their season's goal race.

Competitive adult runners, especially marathoners, typically divide their year into two main seasons. An example of this would be peaking for the Boston Marathon in April, followed by the Chicago Marathon in October. This hypothetical runner will try to be in top shape on the exact day of these two races. To reach this peak, they will go through three to six months of progressively harder training before each marathon.

Runners aim to be in their top physical condition just before the end of a season, but this peak is delicate and can only be maintained for a short window of time. The excessive miles and intensity required to reach an athlete's peak will place significant stress on them. While you must do your best to maintain your health with good recovery habits, the stress from running at your peak training can only be managed for so long. This high level of stress is ultimately relieved through the taper and only then can a top performance come out of you on race day.

Regardless of the outcome of your season's goal race, it is essential to take time off from running afterward. Taking significant rest after a peak performance allows the body to fully heal and benefit long-term from all of the hard work put in during the training season. Rushing too quickly back into running after a peak performance will likely result in performance stagnation, mental burnout, or injury.

Taking time off after a race is as essential as running itself

Schedule time off into your training calendar, just like you do for your base building phase, workout phases, taper, and race dates.

Why you should schedule time off

1. **Overcome performance stagnation** – Taking insufficient rest is one of the top reasons why avid runners do not see improvement. Forcing yourself to take a week or more off after your goal race allows your body to come off of its physical peak and reset to a more natural state. You will only detrain slightly in this time, but your new normal

will be much higher as a result of your hard work in the previous season. When you resume training you will be fully prepared to reach a higher peak before your next goal race.

2. **Avoid mental burnout** – It takes ten years or more to reach your full performance potential in running and you can enjoy running for decades beyond that. Taking a mental break from running several times a year will help you have a long and healthy relationship with the sport. I do not believe it is healthy to be going at full throttle all the time with your training. Running to your potential takes a huge commitment and planned breaks give you time to reflect and prioritize other things for a while. The time off allows you the ability to indulge in other hobbies and focus on those things you may neglect when so much of your energy goes towards your running.

3. **Prevent physical injury** – Excelling at running is all about finding your limit, getting close to it in training, reaching and exceeding it in racing, and then backing off before you go over that limit for too long. Take time off from running after your race to recover completely before you start your next training cycle. This will allow you to come back stronger and more resilient for your next race. Training at

your peak mileage and running a goal race will cause significant stress and potentially even damage to your body whether you realize it or not. Early stages of tendonitis or stress reactions may be present that you are unaware of. You may have been nursing an injury just to get to the starting line. You may have developed a minor injury during the race itself. Force yourself to take time off whether you think you need it or not. It is to your long-term benefit to heal fully before getting back at it.

Do not neglect the importance of the post-race recovery phase or make the mistake of thinking taking time off will make you slow or out of shape. It will not.

Eliud Kipchoge, world record holder in the marathon, has stated he takes several full weeks off after his marathons. If it is good enough for the marathon GOAT, it should be good enough for you too.

It is okay to do some easy exercise during your rest period, but do not put structure to it. Listen to your body and do what sounds fun. Relax more, do not push.

I personally like to go on easy bike rides, take walks, hike, and go kayaking during my time away from running. Use your post-race recovery phase as an opportunity to explore and have unstructured fun. Try something fun and new during this time.

How much time should you take off after a season's goal race?

Race Distance	Suggested Time Off Running
Marathon (26.2)	2 Weeks Off
Half Marathon (13.1)	1-2 Weeks Off
5K , 10K , or Shorter Event	1-2 Weeks Off
Ultra Marathon (50K+)	2-3 Weeks Off

Note: Every athlete is different. Ask your coach how much time you should take off after your next race. Running a marathon or ultra marathons can cause significant muscular and immune system damage. You may need a month or more of rest and light exercise before you feel back to normal.

The role of a coach in an athlete's recovery

As a coach of both adult and high school athletes, it is my practice to always assign a week or more of rest at the end of every season. As athletes, we tend to think in the short term and often go against what we know is best. I have the long-term health, enjoyment, and performance gains of all my athletes in mind and would never willingly sacrifice their longevity in running by eliminating the post-race recovery phase. While it may sometimes feel like an unnecessary or forced break, runners will always benefit long term from taking time off after a race.

Supplemental Practices
To Go Beyond
"Just Running"

1. Strength Training Guide

Who is this guide for?

This strength training guide is intended for the distance runner who wants to improve their performance in the 5K to marathon. For best results, this guide is meant to supplement an athlete's running-focused training program.

Personalize these strength training routines by substituting in exercises you enjoy or that target specific areas that have troubled you in the past.

The given exercises, times, reps, and sets are something to work towards. Build up to them gradually and once they become too easy, consider doing more challenging exercises for further your strength development.

When should I strength train?

If running is your primary sport, strength training is best done after your running is finished for the day. Complete your strength training either immediately after finishing your run or later in the day, depending on your preference. Remember to hydrate and consider taking in some calories between the run and strength training, especially if your total exercise session is over 60 minutes.

Perform the majority of your strength training on your harder running days so your easy days are more restful. Alternatively, you may prefer to perform shorter sessions of strength training after every run.

Why should I strength train?

Strength training for runners is primarily meant as pre-hab against possible running-related injury to allow you to run more consistently. Strength training gives your body the capacity to handle higher mileage and intensity. For example, by regularly strength training, you may be able to safely handle ten extra miles or one extra workout each week.

Strength training helps you maintain your running form during challenging long runs, workouts, and races. While strength training can be used to maintain fitness during periods of decreased running or injury, it is not a substitute for running itself. If all is going well with your running training, then strength training should never be used in place of mileage or running workouts.

Tips for strength training

While runners are typically great at running, often we are not as interested in performing strength training exercises. Here are some tips to make strengthening a fun and consistent part of your weekly plan:

- Write strength training into your weekly plan, just like you do with your mileage and workout specifics.

- Have a coach, teammate, or friend hold you accountable to completing your strength training.

- If you are short on time, end your run one mile short so you can spend five to ten minutes strength training and do not worry about missing one mile.

- Strength train outside. I often run into a park with exercise equipment or playground structures that can be used as a gym mid-run or towards the end of one. As a bonus, completing your strength training before heading back indoors is a great way to make sure it gets done.

- Play music or listen to an audiobook or podcast while you strength train.

- Set goals and challenges for your strength training, just like you do for your running. How long can you hold a plank? How many push ups can you do? Can you get strong enough to complete your first pull-up?

How much strength training should I do?

My general recommendation for most distance runners is to gradually build your strength routines until you are training two to three times per week for fifteen to thirty minutes at a time.

Start with body weight exercises like those described in this chapter. Once these become easy, you can either keep doing them or choose to level-up to performing exercises with external weights. Weight training is not necessary to be a strong runner, but for those who enjoy strength work or are looking for more variety over time, weights make a great addition to a training program.

Knighton Runs "Pre-Run" Strength and Mobility Routine

Perform immediately before starting an easy or long run.

Time Required = 3 to 5 minutes

Purpose = Warm-up body before running, build leg strength and stability

5 sec - Arm Swings Forwards and Backwards

5 sec - Standing Hip Rotations Clockwise

5 sec - Standing Hip Rotations Counter-Clockwise

6x Pull Knee to Chest (3x each leg)

6x Pull Heel to Butt (3x each leg)

10x Reach up Tall then Touch Alternating Toes (5x each side)

10x Forward Lunge (5x each leg)

10x Lunge with a Twist (5x each leg)

10x Side Lunge (5x each side)

10x Back and To The Side Lunge (5x each side)

10x Back Lunge (5x each leg)

20x Leg Swings Front to Back (10x each leg)

20x Leg Swings Side to Side (10x each leg)

Walk for 10 to 30 seconds then begin your run.

Knighton Runs "Post-Run" Strength and Mobility Routine

Perform immediately after completing your run.

Step 1: Circuit Exercises

Time Required = 5 to 10 minutes

Purpose = Strengthen upper body, core, and legs

12x Push up

12x Dip

12x Superman Row

12x Leg Raise (laying on back)

12x Double Leg Glute Bridge

12x Bowler Squat on Left Leg

12x Bowler Squat on Right Leg

Complete 1 set on an easy day, 2 on a hard day

Step 2: Planks

Time Required = 3 minutes

Purpose = Improve full-body and core strength

Front Plank (work up to 60 seconds)

Right-Side Plank (work up to 30 seconds)

Left-Side Plank (work up to 30 seconds)

Reverse Plank (work up to 30 seconds)

Step 3: 7-Way Hips

Time Required = 6 minutes

Purpose = Strengthen and Stabilize the Hips

Lay on one side of your body, perform the following exercises, moving from the hip:

12x Lateral Leg Raise

12x Forward Leg Swing

12x Backward Leg Swing

12x Full Leg Swings (back and forth)

12x Clockwise Circles

12x Counter-Clockwise Circles

12x Forward Knee Drive

Then switch sides and repeat with the opposite leg.

Lower Leg Strengthening Routine

Running puts a lot of stress on your lower legs, ankles, and feet. New runners are especially susceptible to developing shin splints and other lower leg injuries if their muscles, tendons, and bone tissue become overworked before they adapt to their increased training regimen.

To help prevent shin splints and other lower leg injuries, ensure any increases to your mileage and intensity are made gradually. Rotate your shoes daily and run on soft surfaces as much as possible. Additionally, performing lower leg strengthening exercises like the routine below may help reduce your risk of developing a lower leg injury.

The following routine should be performed after every run.

Time Required = 2 minutes
Purpose = Strengthen lower legs and feet

With Shoes On:
10 sec - Walk on heels with toes pulled up and back

With Shoes Off:
10 sec - Walk on tip-toes
10 sec - Walk on insides of feet
10 sec - Walk on outsides of feet
10 sec - Walk with toes pointed inward
10 sec - Walk with toes pointed outward
10 sec - Walk on tip-toes backwards
10x calf raises with toes pointed forward
10x calf raises with toes pointed inward
10x calf raises with toes pointed outward

2. Post-Run Stretching

There are two types of stretching you need to know about: dynamic and static.

Dynamic stretching includes the briefly held stretches and range of motion exercises you perform in your warm up. Dynamic stretching is discussed elsewhere in this book. Static stretching exercises are the longer holds that loosen tight muscles while expanding range of motion. Static stretching will be discussed here.

When I first started running, I did not stretch. Why bother? But a few years ago, I began to perform static stretches after most of my runs and I immediately noticed a big difference in my recovery.

I find static stretching after running helps with my flexibility, range of motion, and keeps my muscles from getting tight. It also just feels good, especially now that I am getting older.

The science on static stretching for distance runners seems to be a mixed bag. Some say it is good, while others say it does not matter. Some even think it can be detrimental. As a coach, I think if it feels good and helps you relax, it is worth doing. Recovery in many ways is more mental than physical. If we believe it works, then it most likely does.

Static stretching is one of those aspects of training that seems to be optional, but for some can be a game changer. It is worth experimenting with to find what works best for you.

Tips for static stretching

- Perform static stretching only after your run is complete.

- Stretch before your muscles cool down. Warm muscles stretch better.

- Hold each stretch for eight to ten seconds, or until you feel a good stretch with increased range of motion.

- Perform each stretch twice.

- If the area being stretched becomes numb or is painful, back off.

My favorite post-run stretches

Figure-4 Gluteal Stretch

Sit-and-Reach Hamstring Stretch

Hamstring Stretch, laying on back

Instep Stretch / Runner's Lunge

Standing Calf Stretch

(Tip: This one is easy to do at the kitchen counter
or in the shower after you run)

Butterfly Sitting Groin Stretch

Additionally, many yoga postures and flows feel great for runners. Taking a weekly yoga-for-runners class can be a helpful practice and is a great thing to do on a rest day. Some of my best running came in the times when I was attending a hot yoga class every Sunday.

Overall, my motto for post-run stretching is simple, *"if it feels good, do it. If it doesn't, don't."* Experiment to find what makes you feel the best and recover faster.

3. Accelerating Recovery with Massage

Self-massage tools give distance runners a big advantage when it comes to preventing and recovering from injury. Massage may help improve your flexibility, increase your range of motion, reduce your muscle tension, and decrease the recovery time between your workouts. In a perfect world, I would have a massage therapist who would instantly appear the moment I had an achy back, sore shoulders, or painfully tight IT bands. While many professional athletes are lucky enough to enjoy this luxury, most everyday runners are not.

That is where self-massage tools work wonders. I have spent years acquiring an arsenal of tools that help work out my sore spots. I believe that regular use of these tools can also help prevent us from getting sore or injured in many cases as well.

The key is finding the right self-massage tools for your needs. While many athletes can get away with just one all-purpose tool to rub and flush their muscles, I own different tools that each address a more specific need.

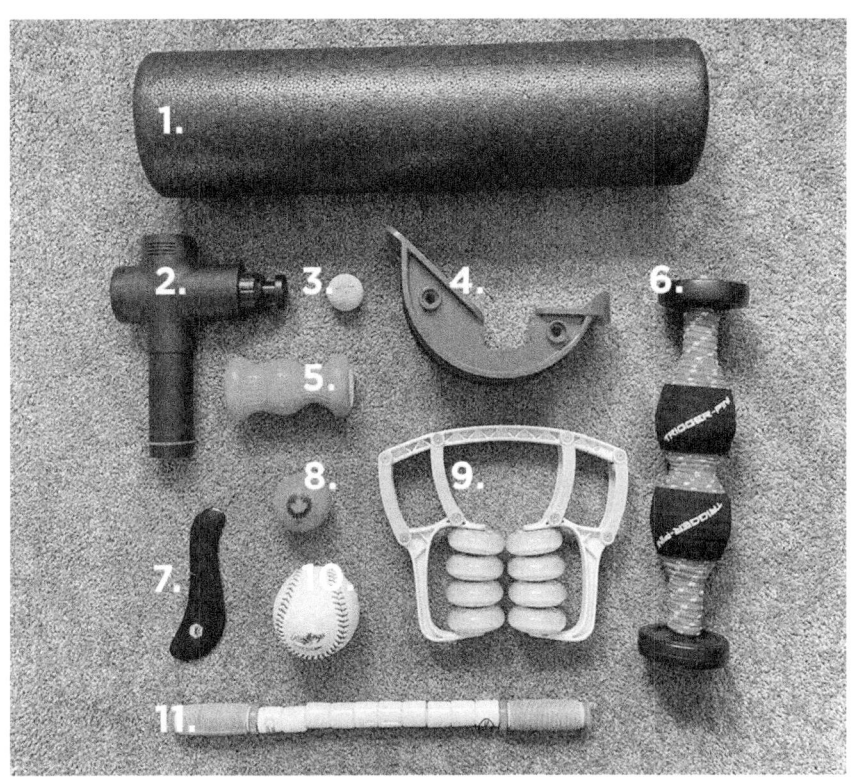

These are the self-massage tools I use on a regular basis to keep me running injury-free:

1. **Foam Roller**

   A staple for all athletes. If you ask a runner friend what to do about your achy IT band chances are they will say, *"try foam rolling."* Foam rollers are cheap and simple. They're old school and somewhat awkward, but they do the job.

2. **Portable Massage Gun**

   Massage guns are increasing in popularity and I will admit I jumped on the bandwagon here. However, the high price of some of the name brand models gave me serious sticker shock. I opted for this much less expensive version. It is quite a bit louder than its competitors, but it gets the job done. Personally, I just do not see the value in the name-brand products which are four to six times the price of the generic models.

3. **Golf Ball**

   A golf ball is perfect for travel and can get into those pinpoint spots that need a lot of pressure. Just be careful not to go too hard when using a golf ball or you might bruise.

4. **Calf Stretcher**

   This is one of my oldest tools. If you have chronically tight calves as I do, this stretcher will be your new best friend. It helps relieve and stretch the plantar fascia, calf, foot, and hamstring muscles far more effectively than conventional methods.

5. **Foot Roller**

   A foot roller is another great option for rolling out achy arches and plantar fascia. This one is great to toss in your travel bag to bring to a race.

6. **Pin Roller**

   I picked this one up at the Boston Marathon Expo quite a few years ago and to be honest I do not think this specific one is still being made. I can tell you that this is the most painful tool we own. With that said, it is great for a sore back or a really tight IT band. Desperate times call for desperate measures.

7. **Scraper Tool**

   If you have ever had the Graston Technique performed on you then you already know the torment and bliss of a scraper tool. This incredible tool works by providing myofascial release to your problem areas. By breaking up scar tissue and adhesions just beneath the skin you can restore blood flow to problem areas. Not only does this reduce pain, but it also improves overall mobility.

8. **Bike Polo Ball**

   From my glory days as a semi-professional bike polo player, this hard red ball can work wonders on a sore hamstring. If you can not get into a bike polo tourney very easily enough to snag one, a lacrosse ball makes for a good alternative. I also like to keep a softer tennis ball in our car for long rides. This way I can fit in a little extra self care while on the go.

9. **Clamp-Style Roller**

    This is the go-to tool in the Knighton household. You can literally use this one while sitting on the couch and it is not nearly as scary as it looks. This roller clamps on your leg muscles and can work them all by simply rolling it back and forth.

10. **Softball**

    If you want to go big or go home, you can use a softball to dig into that hammy just the way you might with a lax ball or tennis ball. If the pinpoint pressure from smaller balls is too intense for you, a softball can make for a great option.

11. **Stick Roller**

    Sticks travel well and can be used on almost every area of the body without having to lay awkwardly on the floor. Great for rolling out tight calves, this is a good tool to put in your travel bag and use before a race.

4. Choosing Running Shoes

Just like how every run should have a purpose, every shoe you own should have a purpose as well. When your type of shoe matches the type of run you are doing, you'll train better and more smoothly.

It is true that you can do all of your running in the same pair of shoes, but it is not optimal. For many beginner runners, starting with one pair of shoes makes sense because the outlay of cash for five or more different styles of shoes can be prohibitive and unnecessary at first. But as you become more committed to the sport, you should strongly consider purchasing a different style of shoe halfway through the life of your current model until your running shoe quiver is full.

Performance-driven runners do not repeat the same type of run for multiple days on end when following their training plans, and so too should their types of shoes rotate throughout the week as well.

Avoid wearing the same pair of running shoes twice in a row. This will distribute wear more evenly on your shoes and help them last longer. By rotating shoes you may even help reduce your injury risk by mixing up the impact forces and movement patterns your body experiences throughout the week.

The main types of shoes you should have in your quiver are:

1. Easy Day Shoes
2. Recovery Day Shoes
3. Trail Running Shoes
4. Long Run Shoes
5. Workout Shoes
6. Race Shoes

Test out different brands and models of shoes until you find your favorites. Once you find a pair that works well for you, consider buying multiple pairs of that model to ensure you have access to it for a year or two, or even longer. Running shoe models get updated constantly by manufacturers and often a shoe you like will not be available for very long.

Easy day shoes

Think of your easy day shoes as your average, everyday shoe. They also have got to become your best friend. You will wear these running shoes the most. If you are just starting out running, this is the pair you should buy first with. These everyday trainers are typically medium-weight, medium-cushion, and lower cost. While you can do workouts and races in these shoes, they are not built specifically for the job.

Easy day shoes are great for twenty to ninety minute runs at comfortable to moderate intensity levels and work equally well on roads or trails. If the weather is poor, these are probably the shoes you do not care too much about getting messy. It is helpful to own two models of easy day shoes so that you always have a dry pair ready to go before your next run.

Recovery day shoes

Recovery Day shoes are a lot like easy day shoes, but with a couple of distinctive factors. Having extra cushion in your recovery day shoe will give a less jarring ride during your slow 30 to 60 minute recovery jogs. Having a shoe you are comfortable taking off-road is also helpful in a recovery day shoe since recovery days are best run off pavement.

In some cases, a recovery day shoe can double as a long run or even a highly cushioned workout shoe. The key is having an extremely comfortable shoe that you can rotate into throughout the week for slow, healing jogs. The goal of a recovery run is to end it feeling better than you started. The right shoe choice can help promote this feeling on a recovery day.

Trail running shoes

Every runner who is serious about improving should own at least one pair of trail shoes. Running on soft surfaces should make up at least 50% of your mileage and trail shoes are meant for this! While road running shoes work perfectly well in most unpaved conditions, having a dedicated trail shoe can be helpful in wet conditions and make you feel more confident running off-road.

Trail shoes run the gamut from light-weight racers to chunky trainers and everything in between. Start off with a medium-to-high cushioned, light-weight trail shoe. This style of shoe will serve you well both off and on the pavement.

Workout and racing shoes

These shoes are meant for going fast! To achieve your best performance on a workout or race day, you need a shoe that is fit for the job. These shoes are typically very lightweight and their shapes promote running with better form.

Historically workout and race shoes were low-cushion for less weight and a better ground feel. Modern workout and race shoes tend to have more cushion and less ground feel as midsole foam technology has improved. Despite high-stack foamy shoes being the new norm for road races, there is still a place for the minimalist racing flat and spike in your rotation.

In general, workout and race shoes should be reserved for fast running only. Only put them on after you warm up and take them off before you cool down.

There are three main types of workout or race shoes: racing flats, track and cross country spikes, and carbon-plated super shoes.

Racing flats

Racing flats are best for training at mile pace, 5K, 10K, and half marathon pace on the road or track. They could be worn for marathon-pace training but usually would not be comfortable enough to wear for a full 26.2 miles. These lightweight, thin-soled shoes are great for feeling fast and nailing tough workouts. Historically these were also the fastest road-race shoes for distances 5K and up, but modern carbon-fiber shoe technologies have one-upped them. That said, they still hold a place in every serious runner's quiver for fast workouts due to the natural footstrike and stride they encourage.

Track and cross country spikes

Track spikes are meant for training and racing on the track when raw speed is the ultimate concern. Cross Country (XC) spikes are very similar but designed for running on grass or trail cross country courses. Cushion and upper frills are sacrificed for weight savings in these shoes, though modern ones can be surprisingly comfortable. There are special spikes for just about every event. If you do not race on the track or XC, you probably will never need a pair. But if you want to run your best in these disciplines, or just want to try something fun and different, give a pair of spikes a try.

Carbon-plated super foam shoes

In 2017, Nike released the Nike Vaporfly 4% shoe and completely changed the road running world as we knew it. The 4% shoe and now subsequent editions by Nike and their competitors provide a significant advantage over traditional racing flats. Seemingly every world record on the roads and track has fallen in recent years from athletes wearing this new type of shoe and even the most casual runner will see a huge improvement in their times when wearing them.

Despite these shoes providing a clear advantage, even being considered mechanical-doping by many, most models are legal in competition. For better or worse, if you do not wear a carbon-plated super foam shoe during a distance race today, you are on an uneven playing ground against your competitors.

The advantage of super shoes lies primarily in the revolutionary midsole foam they use. Their supreme cushioning combined with their low weight allows runners to run much faster and with minimal fatigue when compared to traditional racing flats.

On the negative side, these shoes are typically very expensive when compared to training shoes and have poor durability. Additionally, their high-stack heights and the squishiness of their midsoles can force athletes into running with an unusual form. Therefore most athletes save them for races or only the most important workouts.

A note on fair competition

While all shoe models are fair game in training, running's governing bodies have established rules regarding stack-heights of shoes for both track and road competitions. These rules were put in place to prevent the new shoe technologies from getting totally out of hand. In both professional and amateur running, what was once considered a good time is already just average due to the recent changes in shoe technology. As mentioned earlier, the record books have been rewritten largely due to these shoes alone.

Despite these new rules, shoe companies are now making models of shoes that are illegal in certain types of competition. Please respect the rich history and rules of our sport by only wearing competition-legal shoes in your races. Times, finishing order, and PR's set when wearing illegal shoes or violating other rules of competition do not count.

Putting Theory Into Action

You now know the essential principles of marathon training, but what will you do with this information?

Putting theory into action is how you turn your knowledge into reality.

You become the average of the people you spend the most amount of time with. If you want to become a better runner, one of the best ways to do this is to get involved with a running community. Find others to train alongside, support each other, and let your combined efforts uplift the whole team.

Nowadays it is very easy to find a running community that appeals to you either in person or online. There is no need to go it alone.

For many adult athletes, working with a running coach gives them that extra push they need to become their best. Despite the fact that every sports team and nearly all professional runners have a coach, many passionate adult athletes try to go it alone. While this may work for some, I am constantly blown away by how positively impactful the coaching relationship is for my adult athletes.

The benefits you will receive from training well and excelling in running go far beyond just earning faster times on paper. When you succeed as an athlete, you develop the skills to accomplish anything that you set your heart and mind towards.

Your full potential is unknown.

For additional resources, training plans, and coaching services, visit my website at www.knightonruns.com

Goal Setting Exercise

1. Why Do You Run?

Write your top 3 most powerful reasons.

2. Short-Term Goal Setting

Write your most important goal for 3 to 6 months from today.

3. Medium-Term Goal Setting

Write your most important goal for 1 to 2 years from today.

4. Long-Term Goal Setting

What do you want to have accomplished 5 years from today?

5. Record 1 Take-Away From This Book

What will you implement into your running right away?

6. Hold Yourself Accountable

How will you ensure you do what it takes to reach your goals?

Notes